This series prepared in consultation with the British Veterinary Association Animal Welfare Foundation

First published 1990 by
Campbell Books
96 Leonard St · London EC2A 4RH
in association with The Watts Group

ISBN 1 85292 052 1
Printed in Singapore
10 9 8 7 6 5 4 3 2 1

We have a
Guinea pig

Rod Campbell

CAMPBELL BOOKS

We have a guinea pig.
I love it very much and
like helping to look
after it . . .

My guinea pig needs two
meals a day.
I help to feed it fresh
green food, and grains,
and hay.

Sometimes I give my
guinea pig special treats
like sunflower seeds,
nuts, and raisins.
I never give it chocolates
or sweets.

sunflower seeds

nuts

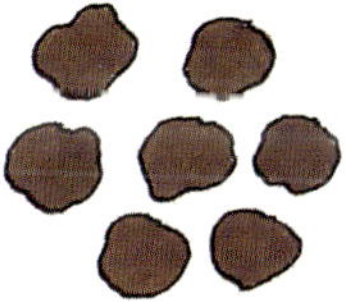

raisins

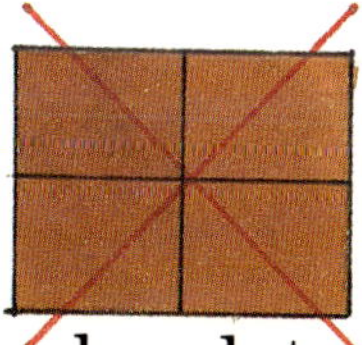

chocolate

sweets

My guinea pig lives outside in a special hutch. The hutch has a warm dry sleeping part with hay and straw, and a living area.

When I pick up my guinea pig I do so very carefully, like this . . .

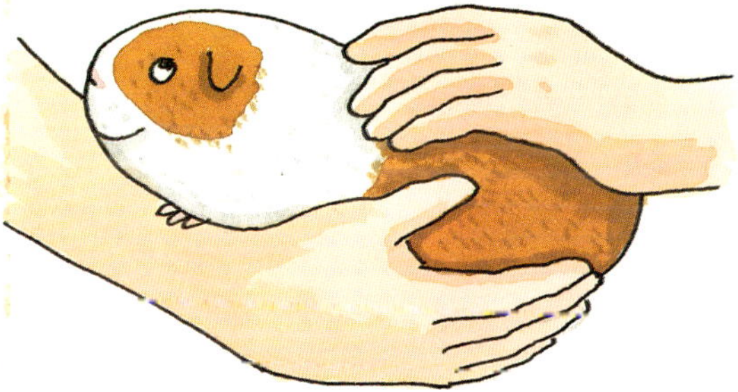

I help to clean my
guinea pig's hutch every
day, and wash it out
once a week.
I put in clean straw
for it to sleep on.

To keep my guinea pig well, we always visit the Vet.
The Vet is the animals' doctor.

My guinea pig has gone
to bed.

Can you see it in the hutch?
Shh…don't wake it up!